I0162981

NO ENTRY

Poems: M SARKI

PREVIOUS POETRY COLLECTIONS:

Zimble Zamble Zumble
Little War Machine
Mewl House

NO ENTRY © 2014 M S A R K I

PUBLISHED BY
THE ROGUE LITERARY SOCIETY
LOUISVILLE, KY

ISBN-13: 978-0692297018 (Rogue Literary Society)
ISBN-10: 0692297014

PRINTED IN THE USA
ALL RIGHTS RESERVED

COVER ART, BOOK DESIGN & LAYOUT
© 2014 ROGUE LITERARY SOCIETY

NO ENTRY by M Sarki was originally published in 2012
by *Ravenna Press,* Edmonds, WA as part of a limited
paperback trade edition titled *TRIPLE #2* . Each
publication of the *Triple Series* features separate
collections by three different authors.

DEDICATION

For BeverlyLane and Gordon Lish

"Every thought is already a tribe, the opposite of a state."

_____Gilles Deleuze and Felix Guattari
From *NOMADOLOGY*

INTRODUCTION
by M Sarki

Absent an overweening attitude for a groundless literary success it still behooves me to comment briefly on matters regarding *No Entry*, a small book of mine previously included in the second installment in the *Ravenna Triple Series*. Paired with the gifted writers, Kathryn Rantala and Harold Bowes, I was afforded the liberty and place-setting of going first with my say in the second offering in this new series of books erupting out of the great northwestern state of Washington. Having written for *Ravenna Press* the introduction to my section titled *No Entry* almost a year to the day of receiving the actual book in the mail I really had no remembrance of what I had previously written those many months ago. I was surprised. And that is a good thing, being surprised by your own work and sharing no little measure of delight in it. Such is the grim fact that this feeling doesn't happen often enough. But today I was pleased with what I had to say now almost two years ago, the praise I spread all over the names of those people closest to me who had helped me so much along my literary way, and the realization that in the introduction I wasn't at all sloppily sentimental. Given my state of emotions at play back then I was thrilled I had behaved somewhat admirably. Having returned from the Humpty Dumpty dead was one thing, but finding myself back in print with the likes of my old brothers and sisters was clearly an event I would never take lightly. Even the twenty-nine poems I included in this collection, and arranged chronologically from early 1996 through 2011, were better than I had remembered them being and wondered at where they came from. *Who was that person?*

For half of my adult life I toiled as a carpenter and the latter half spent less rigorously in a sales position providing the products that builders need. About four years ago, near the end of that second career, I fell off another roof almost a decade after my first introduction to real pain. The fall in my earlier initiation broke, instead of me, several clay pots and instantly, though temporary, made it such that I could not breathe. Ten years later I fell from my cabin roof and broke my left arm and right leg, also destroying my knee in the process. Three ambulance rides and three hospitals later I landed in the care of the gifted surgeon who could actually put me back together. Trauma is an easy word to discount and is routinely misunderstood until you've had a personal and intimate experience with it. I spent two months in a wheelchair, another two months using a walker, and then a cane for another five months before I had the ability and confidence to walk with no aid. When something catastrophic occurs, and you have first-hand experience of it, there is a shift in every direction. I was not sure if I would ever write a poem again, or read a book, or even watch a film from beginning to end. Because of the physical and emotional upheaval done to my body, along with the narcotics ingested to help control it, it was very hard to focus. Little by little I regained my faculties, my physical liabilities lessened, and I was back to making any kind of art I could.

The twenty-nine poems that chronologically follow here reach from as early as the late 1990's up to the year 2011. It is not surprising to me that my grandfather on my father's side plays a very active role in these poems as does my wife of thirty-one years. Both of these people, Charles Sarki and Beverly Lane, were, and are, the greatest. Beverly and I had a son together, and I credit Evan Sarki for the title of a poem I have included in this collection. Many years ago he made a Mother's Day card, most likely in kindergarten or before, and on it, with stick drawings of his mother and he, were the words, "I am thanked by you for having me".

_____*M Sarki*
Louisville, Kentucky
18 September 2014

CONTENTS

NO ENTRY

Poems: M SARKI

Effacing the Clown

It was the strangest goose
was going. Rugged and
bad to sneak into

the pasture
with the rabbits.
And an eaglet

on the ground
being devoured by
a cat.

1

On the Favor of the Lost

It fits the crime
so beautifully.
The long angles

gleaming in the
claque of its twilight.
Its old bosoms suffocating

this joyous occasion.
And the renderings they
hang as being still

compossible to us.
All this. And nothing
too soon.

Ishpeming Is Freezing

Back in the hold and
hidden by other matters
comes the faint

banter of uncalloused
feet. Else haunts the
restless shroud

caught in winter's
madness. But to scurry
forth should favor then

torn muscles of the
midnight. Books made
by radical occasion.

Leather briefs. The
hunt that seems fair.

Wretched Paint of the Latter Houses

He marshals every
precinct made,
occasions kindness

spent. Peels away
their underpinnings,
hugs them to his

chest. Orders court
and teedles some,
de-boots the

young, bestrides.
And still he is
a judge forlorn,

exhausted
but alive.

Being Thanked by You for Having Me

I am a jacatoo.
Indulgent in my
stuttering. And

your admonishments
pronounce me
clumsy. But it

is I who twills
my strategies.
Delayed, yes.

But full of note.
And void
of compromise.

5

My Finnish Grandfather

He was in the
vicinity of nobody
most of the time.

Out in his scraggly
berry patch or
on his knees

with his carrots
and weeds in
the sand he

called his garden.
He mined gypsum
ore and was

thought to be
dangerous. But
I believed he was

the U.S. Calvary.
Not Cavalry, tyhmä.

Forward: An Interview with God

I remember winter's
river being lunar
and frigid. My

tip-ups drowning
under the clime of
icy domes. Those

wily pike beneath
them smiling as if
they had it better

than I did up here.

7

A Pinchcock Adored

There was
no dulling my
confusion, so

you taught me
to build a boat.
To gather seeds

and determine
suitable places
in which to lodge

them. I look back
now and see the
depressions I

made. The
shovels and hoes
as counterfeit

billies. The
spineless drag
on shore.

Above the Plankton

It was climbing
onto Noah. A
fontanel of dew

at the stern of
his neck. The
moment beyond

reckoning.
Another tote
on board.

Once, for Leaving Holland

Having done
in you, lately,
the spectacular.

Returning, again,
from the goings-on
of our chronic glut.

10

The Ditch

Our drift
was prone
to atrophy.

A stick,
without a sail,
maligned.

And hunger
nagged our
awful home,

the sun our
feral sky.

11

Long after Helen Died

That meadow makes duty out
of cantering.

And for writing
down with
the birds

behind his
singing kettle.
He notes

the dumb implements.
Their extinct

designs.
The time
he spends

maneuvering.

Hastening to Make Waste

In the moonlight
she is vigorous.
Her flesh

attends to
the weight of
her marriage.

The three of us
collide. What
astounding

wreckage.

13

Square Cap for Minnie

It did not commence with
my receiving a letter in the
mail from my book pal,
Slingest. No, these
advances began years
before with postal
deliveries of photographs
of his naked wife and,
every so often, a poem of
the first rank. He certainly
meant to get my attention,
not to mention Stevens
turning to turn out verses
as none other had before
him. He wanted me to do
it, Slingest did, to his wife.
Must have believed a
poem beside the point.

14

Bad News in the Belly

My sister whispered
kiss me as we tumbled
down the crag,

trapped in a wooden
guard nailed crudely
to our vests, her

sweaty muscles
bursting through the
slats, which might

have split into, oh,
inexpressibly argute
shards, and into

other vagaries,
perhaps.

15

Copen

She smelled a
broken glass
of flowers

wilting near
her tree.
Tossed to

the ground
above whose roots
the petals

turned to seed.
That someone
cared about

them once,
and closed them
to his chest,

is proof who
loves a blossom
more gives

yes to violets.

Dirty Painted Flowers

My hackle
is this pug
mill sawlshot.

Its use beyond
profane. A
groveling

mihungtang
of sordid
proportion.

And all
that remains.

17

National City

There is solace
in this dry pine air,
the sunlight streaming

through the tall oaks
standing sentinel
around our cabin.

We sit in plastic
chairs and turn
our cheeks to

the rushing summer.
Our bare toes squeezing
this hot lawn of sand,

wishing for more
tomorrows and
thinking, yes,

more of the same.
Yes, more of the same.

Onward Christian Soldier

On the last day
he measured rope.
And shortened it.

There was nothing
she could do. Some
accused him of losing

his mind. Others didn't.
It was his life, they said.
There were too many

rocks in it. He remembered
the ice of Lake Huron. The
pier and Red Cross.

The incessant push his
mother made while
strangling him.

The Tools of Migrant Hunters

There is a half note
fighting to be heard.
The furtive lurching

of a stranded time
wandering adrift and
deserted, ravaged by

the loss of our interest
in savages. But the
cry the wolf makes

still muffles the
fumbling in the reading
of our passages.

The rules laid down
by men. The ranting
and raving of lunatics.

20

How I Met My Wife

The lamplight crows its insolence.
Before me rest two chairs. They
appear not to be for sitting. A
woman from the market has
removed her clothes. She emits
some radiance never witnessed
before. And the crowd that
multiplies makes standard her
procedures. She is determined to
satisfy, if not the hoard of
onlookers then at least the man she
came for. Not once do I lose her
eyes staring at me, directing my
leave of the audience. Crafting
disbelief into miracle.

21

Stripping the Wax from That Photograph

A better man would have saved you.
Hoisted you on his back and
climbed the rotten stairs.

Measured the distance and range
of difficulty as suitable for
your deliverance from

this world and where you
thought you were going.
One more breath of

fresh air and a look about the
horizon. One last chance
for me to show I cared

and to prove again
I love you.

Comments a Brother Makes

The gravel side closed
in the dust of his coming.
Fourteen days without

a drop of rain. Torn
soles and leather tops
crumbling between

the cracks of his toes.
There was little question
he was a serious man.

Going places. Or
heading somewhere
only he could know.

As if his journey
depended on him as
its only load. As

if it really mattered.

Hearts in Flood

The rest of your clean laundry
was pressed into bags bearing
your name on them and
whatever else we could use
to describe you accurately.
Your survivors wanted more,
of course, as if our answers
could save them. We simply
added that war isn't pretty,
and pinned a bright medal to
your chest, or what remained
of it.

24

For Beverly, Between the Pages

Where you cheated was yourself.
The burden on your back for being
beautiful. The men and boys

afraid to ask you for your favors
in a way so unacceptable, even if
they did. The proof in later years

that he was right about his love
for you and what was missing.
The time you both took to make

a new history. The kind that
finds its way into a book.

Waiting for Noon

Hiding behind
the wizard's crown
are the colors of

her whistle. She
has always favored
corbeau and scab,

and so dismisses
the nuns and what
is acceptable to their

order. A permanent
mark upon her, she
blows it anyhow.

Getting a Wink of Dandy

I tell a story too late for words.
Better left to pictures and something
less sanctimonious. A religion

unkempt and verging on pornography.
A wife who does not weep at
injustices, but rather asks for more

of the same. Who wonders what
you've got, hidden there behind the
lamp post, solo in your raincoat,

caught in our sick town.

27

Sam Who Swings the Long Pole

Place the lantern on the shelf
above the dead kok and coal
ready for the stove. It is a

wonder how these buggers
get in here. Took me years
to get used to seeing them

on their sides, eyes wide open,
and with those lofty stares. The
fuel came from a cellar store

found in an abandoned home
in downtown Oscoda. Rats
and coom somehow go together

with greasy spoons and salmon
fishing. In this town your
mouth starts there.

28

No Entry

In the morning,
your bedclothes
wet with fallen

sleep, I slip
into the crease
he made for you.

And where
justice plays
its reel of film

for all the
world to see.

www.ingramcontent.com/pod-product-compliance
Lightning Source LLC
Chambersburg PA
CBHW060045050426
42448CB00012B/3125